WRESTLINGS, WONDERS AND WANDERERS!

Sermons For Pentecost (First Third)
Cycle A First Lesson Texts

BY JUSTIN W. TULL

C.S.S. Publishing Co., Inc.
Lima, Ohio

WRESTLINGS, WONDERS AND WANDERERS!

Scripture quotations are from the *New Revised Standard Version of the Bible,* copyright 1989 by the Division of Christian Education of the National Council of the Churches of Christ in the USA. Used by permission.

Library of Congress Cataloging-in-Publication Data

Tull, Justin W., 1945-
    Wrestlings, wonders and wanderers! : sermons for Pentecost (first third), cycle A first lesson texts / by Justin W. Tull.
        p.   cm.
    ISBN 1-55673-430-1
    1. Pentecost season — Sermons.   2. Bibles. O.T. — Sermons.   3. United Methodist Church (U.S.) — Sermons.   4. Methodist Church — Sermons.   5. Sermons, American.   I. Title
BV4300.5.T85   1992
252'.6—dc20   92-5207
                                                                                         CIP

9233 / ISBN 1-55673-430-1   PRINTED IN U.S.A.

This book is dedicated to Dr. W.J.A. Power who was the first to make the Old Testament stories come alive for me.

Table Of Contents

Preface

This book is a collection of sermons based on the Old Testament readings of the Common Lectionary beginning with Pentecost Sunday. These readings are a treasure house of stories about our ancient forefathers — people like Abraham, Jacob, Esau, Joseph and Moses. I have titled this collection of sermons *Wrestlings, Wonders and Wanderers!* They collectively reflect a myriad of human struggles, the wonders of God's presence and power and the adventuresome journey required of the people of God. If we are to be faithful Christians today, we, too, must face our share of struggles and find in the divine promises of old, new hope for our future and that of our world.

I am indebted to so many people who have helped to make this book possible. To my wife, Lynn, I owe my gratitude for her constant support of my ministry and her careful labor in making final corrections to my manuscript. I am also most grateful to Jean Merritt who graciously and painstakingly scrutinized every word and phrase of the manuscript, offering numerous corrections and suggestions. Finally, I am indebted to the staff and membership of two churches, Walnut Hill United Methodist Church, Dallas, Texas, and First United Methodist Church, Denton, Texas, who were the first recipients of these sermons and provided love, support and help during their composition and revisions.

It has been a sacred privilege to wrestle with these ancient texts. They are as relevant as today's newspaper and markedly more hopeful and helpful. Their stories and images are overflowing with insights into human nature and the mysterious workings of God in our world. If we will but hear the messages of these great texts, we will equip ourselves with a faith and a theology that will be sufficient for our own wrestlings and wanderings. If we will but look around us, the wonders of God will be as burning bushes in our midst and we, like Moses, will know for certain that God is with us — just as he promised!

Day of Pentecost
Isaiah 44:1-8

Spirit Full Or Foul?

Today is Pentecost, the celebration of the gift of God's Spirit to the church and to us. And the question we must ask ourselves and the church is this: Are we Spirit full or Spirit foul? In other words, is God's gift to the Hebrews and to the early Christian church a gift we have received or rejected, nurtured or ignored? Is the Spirit of God in us?

In many ways the gift of the Spirit at Pentecost is not an entirely new act of God. The gift of the Spirit is not exclusively a New Testament occurrence. In the book of Isaiah we find the promise of the Spirit, a promise that was fulfilled in part in Old Testament times but came into full bloom on the day of Pentecost.

Today I invite you on a journey through time, a journey that begins with the ancient days of Isaiah's prophecy. It is a journey tracing the movements of the Spirit as it blows through the community of faith and empowers God's people to be the persons God has created them to be.

We begin with the promise of the Spirit found in Isaiah 44:3b: "I will pour my Spirit upon your descendants, and my blessing on your offspring." The outpouring of the Spirit is thus promised for the future. But indeed the Spirit of God is denied to no person and at no time. Earlier in Isaiah it is

9

made clear that God, the Creator, has always had an intimate relationship with his creation. His Spirit has always been offered to them. Isaiah 44:2 reads: "Thus says the Lord who made you, who formed you from the womb and will help you."

So, what Isaiah is promising is neither a first encounter with the Spirit of God nor the last one. He is promising a special outpouring of the Spirit that will empower his people to flourish and to be a blessing to others. This gift of the Spirit is not to make the people "feel good" or to set them apart as special or elite. The thrust of this passage does not seem to be a private religious experience but an evangelistic outreach that will cause many to call upon the God of Jacob, and many to proclaim that indeed there is only one God.

It is not enough that hearts are warmed but rather that they be set on fire with a message and a mission: to declare the marvelous works of God and to profess him only as Lord of the universe. The text from Isaiah suggests not a minimal encounter with the Spirit but an overwhelming juncture of Creator and creature, an empowering that sends forth the people of God to proclaim God's sovereignty and power. So what does this passage have to do with the day of Pentecost? How does Isaiah's day overlap with the day of the Spirit's empowering of the Jerusalem gathering?

Of course, we worship the same God and the same Spirit. Now, however, this Spirit takes its form not only from the identity of the God of Creation but also from the God who was in Christ, the Spirit of the risen Lord. The coming of the Spirit at Pentecost was in fact a manifestation of the Spirit to what Isaiah called "the descendants of Jacob." The words of Isaiah 44 were fulfilled in part with the coming of the mighty winds of the Spirit on the day of Pentecost. And the results of Pentecost were parallel to those in Isaiah: namely that many would call upon the name of the Lord, many would become a part of the community of faith, many now would be able to affirm the claim of the Divine: "I am the first and the last; besides me there is no god."

The message of Isaiah 44 is about an outpouring of the Spirit. The message of Pentecost is precisely the same. Both speak of the importance of God's interaction with the individual. Both speak of the community of faith. Both portray God as the one who empowers us. Both commission us to spread the word concerning the God we worship. Both send us forth not as the blessed elite but as ambassadors and evangelists for the sake of all people.

My question remains: Who are we in this day and age in light of our two texts? Are we Spirit-filled Christians? Are we Spirit full or Spirit foul? Are we Pentecost Christians or ones who have neither gathered to receive the Spirit nor worked to share it? Are we ones who embody the Spirit or ones who impugn it? Are we Spirit full or Spirit foul?

The gathered church has the promise of the Spirit's presence and power. Christ's Spirit is present where two or more are gathered in his name. So, to become a part of the church is to admit to self and others that we need God, we need the nurture of fellow Christians, we need the power of God in order to be who he calls us to be. If that sounds like childhood dependency, then so be it. Whether we are 12 or 70, we need God and others. If we don't believe that, then we are not ready to be a part of God's church. And we are not ready for the Spirit of God.

The church is more than a human institution. The one special ingredient it has is the Spirit. The Spirit has been given to the church. It is there for all who would receive it. Indeed the Spirit is present throughout our world, throughout the universe. Perhaps we need to take a look at the difference between Spirit full and Spirit foul. Which are we? How would we characterize our church?

Several years ago a lady visited the church I was serving. She announced before entering the sanctuary that she had come to see if the Spirit were present in our church. Did I just imagine that her nose was higher than her eyes? Was she herself full of the Spirit or just full of herself?

11

I must confess that I was as quick to judge her as she was to judge us. I did not think she would find the Spirit among us — not because the Spirit was not there, but because her motive seemed to be simply to identify the Spirit (and by her standards) not to "walk in the Spirit" or to embody the Spirit.

I suggest that a church is Spirit full not by signs of its worship, not by its behavior in the pew, but by its witness to the Spirit. Consider the fruit of the Spirit listed in Galatians: ". . . love, joy, peace, patience, kindness, goodness, faithfulness, gentleness, self-control . . . ." Does our church display these characteristics? Do we as individuals demonstrate these qualities? Are we Spirit full or Spirit foul?

One of the things that irritates me about people who judge my spirituality is that they give me a painful reminder that I am truly lacking in spiritual depth and perfection. The fact that they may be hypocrites and self-righteous snobs does not negate the truth of their criticisms. Don't you just hate it when someone you dislike is right about your weaknesses?

When someone calls the church or me "Spirit foul" rather than "Spirit full," I know there is some truth to their assessment. But I also know that these self-appointed spiritualists will be judged by God and not by themselves. I doubt that they themselves are either Spirit full or open to the Spirit blowing in their midst.

What does it mean to be Spirit full? What does it mean to be one of the descendants of Jacob upon whom the Spirit of God has rested? Let me give you an example.

Several years ago a member of the church where I was the youth director told me the story of one of the members there. Her husband had gone to a football game. On his way back he was killed instantly when a drunk driver swerved into his lane and hit him head-on. The drunk driver was not seriously hurt but was hospitalized for observation.

The next morning the widow of the man killed visited the room of the man who had caused her husband's death. She came but for one purpose: to tell him that she did not hold ill feelings towards him. She told him she forgave him and hoped he would be able to forgive himself as well. This saintly lady was Spirit full. She embodied the Spirit of the one who said, "Father, forgive them for they know not what they do."

What is the difference between people who are Spirit full and Spirit foul? You probably can tell by the prayers they pray. Remember the prayer of the tax collector: "Lord, be merciful to me, a sinner?" That was a Spirit-full prayer.

I also remember a youth who seemed to think of herself as being very spiritual as she told us about the power of God working in her life. She told how during drill-team practice she suddenly realized that she had a piece of chicken in between her two front teeth. Since she was at full attention and could not move, she called upon her God to help her. She prayed that God would loosen the piece of chicken. As more a testimony of her piety than of God's power, she related to us that the piece of chicken dislodged and she was spared the embarrassment upon inspection by the first lieutenant.

Now, what do you think? Was she Spirit full or Spirit foul? Is not God more than dental floss?

If we are waiting upon perfection before we can be Spirit full, then none of us will make it. But we can move toward deeper spirituality. We can pray more often. We can gather for worship like those people of Pentecost and be open to the blowing of the Spirit. But we also can be active in those ministries that the Spirit calls us to perform. As we minister in God's name, we will have the Spirit's power with us.

Isaiah spoke of the outpouring of the Spirit. Those gathered at Pentecost experienced the power of God's Spirit in their midst. It was like water to a thirsty land, like words of salvation to a guilt-ridden people, like a commission to spread the truth of the gospel, like a calling to heal and love God's people.

So, have you now decided? Are we a Spirit-full church or a Spirit-foul church? Are we walking in the Spirit ourselves? Do we show the fruit of the Spirit?

If I see that lady coming again to pass judgment, I do not want to greet her. I know that this church has not yet arrived. I also know that I have not obtained spiritual maturity. But how grateful I am that my God does not approach me as though trying to catch me being inadequate! My God approaches me as a loving Father ready to share his Spirit and power.

My suspicion is that you are somewhere between Spirit full and Spirit foul. My suspicion is that we all could use a strong dose of God's Spirit blowing among us. Am I right?

May I suggest we believe the words of Isaiah, that God does empower us and help us? May I suggest that we wait like those faithful Jews in Jerusalem, that we gather expecting the Spirit to come to us? May I suggest that we daily invite the Spirit of the risen Lord to help us embody the fruits of the Spirit?

The Spirit comes to us by its own power, but it always comes if we invite it. So, if we want to be Spirit full we must learn to pray, we must learn to gather and we must learn to invite.

Those who are open then to the Spirit, will you now make this prayer your own.

Come, my Light, and illumine my darkness.
Come, my Life, and revive me from death.
Come, my Physician, and heal my wounds.
Come, Flame of divine love, and burn up the thorns of
my sins, kindling my heart with the flame of thy love.
Come, my King, sit upon the throne of my heart and reign
there.
For thou alone art my King and my Lord. Amen. [1]

Trinity Sunday
Deuteronomy 4:32-40

Just You, Lord

The sermon today asks the questions as to whether we are aware of God's saving acts and if we acknowledge only him as God. In short, we are asking if God truly helps us.

Several years ago, at my sister's wedding, the officiating minister told a story. It was about an Episcopal minister from Africa. The minister's eight-year-old son did not understand his father's actions just before his sermons. He asked his father: "Why do you always kneel when everyone stands to sing the hymn of preparation?" The father replied, "I kneel in prayer to ask God to help me with the sermon." The young boy quickly asked, "Then why doesn't he?"

Our text for today asks the Hebrews if they have observed God helping them. But the one who asks already knows the answer. Listen to Deuteronomy 4 beginning with verse 34:

Or has any god ever attempted to go and take a nation for himself from the midst of another nation, by trials, by signs, by wonders, and by war, by a mighty hand and an outstretched arm, and by great terrors, according to all that the Lord your God did for you in Egypt before your eyes? To you it was shown, that you might know that the Lord is God; there is no other besides him.

15

The action of God in Egypt was a mighty act. God's action was so powerful and so obvious, how could the Hebrews possibly deny that God had helped them? Indeed, how could the Hebrews believe in any other god but the one who had saved them? The writer of Deuteronomy is urging the Hebrews to accept the overwhelming evidence that God has indeed saved them, that there is no other god and that they owe no less than obedience to him.

But the book of Deuteronomy offers only the first act of our play. The New Testament continues God's drama. Here we also ask if any have seen God act. Here we again ask if there are any other gods. Here we ask if God deserves any less than full obedience.

The story of the New Testament does not read like the book of Deuteronomy. God does not come this time in all power. God does not save his people with a mighty hand. God comes not clothed in force but wrapped in swaddling clothes in a manger. He comes not as mighty king but as a vulnerable child.

Deuteronomy tells of plagues and earthquakes, war and a mighty hand; the gospels speak of a babe and shepherds, meekness and danger. And though Jesus does speak with strong authority, though he does demonstrate power through miracles, he does not save his people by physical force but only by the power of his words to pierce the heart.

The Deuteronomist rightly asks the Hebrews if they have observed God through mighty acts. The gospel writers ask that we look with a discerning eye to see further evidence of the mysterious ways in which God acts in human history.

Bishop Peter Storey, in an address to United Methodist preachers in Nashville, reflected on one New Testament passage: Matthew 27:40b-42a. Jesus is on the cross and the crowd taunts him: " 'If you are the Son of God, come down from the cross.' So also the chief priests, with the scribes and elders, mocked him, saying, 'He saved others; he cannot save himself.' " Bishop Storey pointed out the crowd's ignorance: "They did not understand that it was precisely because he was the Son of God that he was on the cross, that he saved others precisely because he would not save himself."[2]

The gospel gives, in fact, a new twist to the God who is seen with the mighty hand in Deuteronomy. The New Testament story does not deny that God intervenes, that God shapes history. But the New Testament warns us that we must look for more subtle signs of God's kingdom as well. God saves us not only through the mighty hand but even as he hangs with pierced hands on a cross!

Bishop Peter Storey also tells of his friend, Bishop Desmond Tutu. Bishop Tutu spoke of a new understanding of power. He said, "When the white man came to South Africa, we had the land and the white man had the Bible. They asked us to pray with them. When we opened our eyes, they had the land and we had the Bible. The problem is they never understood the terrible swap they made."[3]

The disciples had trouble seeing the new way of God's acting. They looked only for the mighty hand, the show of power, the obvious. They wanted a God to once again free them with physical power and might. They wanted a God to deliver them as he had delivered his people from Egypt. What they received was a discipleship of danger and worldly weakness.

I would suggest to you this morning that we may see our God act in both ways today. Some may witness God's intervening dramatically in their life or in the lives of others. They may witness God's power through a miraculous healing or a surprising victory. Some are convinced that a guardian angel has been with them and delivered them from a terrible foe. But others will experience the power of God in the midst of weakness: In failure, in sickness and even in dying. Many will know the power of God when all the signs around seem to point to defeat and abandonment.

But our questions from Deuteronomy are still so relevant: Have we seen the hand of God in our lives? Has God freed us, saved us, delivered us? And have other gods failed to free us and save us? Have we eliminated them one by one? Do we now believe that there is no other god, and that only God deserves our ultimate trust and final obedience?

17

John Wesley was saved as a child from a burning parsonage and always felt that God had delivered him from such a fate because he had a special purpose for him.[4]

Harold Kushner, who wrote *When Bad Things Happen To Good People*, met God intimately through the suffering of his chronically ill son. In this instance, God did not intervene and spare his child, but God did minister to both the son and the father during the prolonged illness.[5]

Perhaps you have experienced God in one of these ways or perhaps in many ways. The question of the Deuteronomist remains: "Have you seen the evidence that God has delivered you, saved you?" Can you say of your God, "There is no other?"

Most of us are quite aware of the many alternatives to believing in a solitary Supreme Being. Our culture offers many substitutes for God. You know them: money, power, pleasure, work, security. And many of us pay tribute to all or some of these gods. But our faith declares that they are nothing when compared to God.

Our faith declares that we are not saved by winning the lottery or the *Reader's Digest* Sweepstakes. Our faith reminds us that worldly power is never complete or guaranteed. We have learned that worldly power has no defense against death or meaninglessness.

Our faith understands that work gives us a sense of accomplishment but we know it does not form the total basis of our self-worth. If we believe it does, then retirement is void of any real meaning and an individual is stripped of all worth as an individual.

But of all our gods, the most seductive is the god of self. Worshiping self means that everything is measured primarily by how it affects us. The self is our god and we seek to revolve the world around us.

But the ironic thing is that we cannot keep everything revolving around us. We do not have enough mass; we don't have that kind of magnetism. We cannot save ourselves. And if we are followers of the Christ, we must not even try to save ourselves. Jesus has amply instructed us: "He who finds his life will lose it, and he who loses his life for my sake will find it (Matthew 10:39)."

Only God can provide the power to keep things in proper orbit. Only God can set the planets in motion and maintain the ongoingness of time. Only God can provide the proper direction for our lives. Only God works as the center, keeping things out of chaos, offering us new freedoms as we revolve around him.

Only God is God! That was the Deuteronomist's claim, and that is our claim as Christians. Some can see that God is God from the mighty hand. Others see the scarred hands of Christ and know of God's love and saving power.

But no matter how we come to believe in the God above all gods, there is but one appropriate response. The Hebrews rightly said it was to follow the commandments. Jesus said it was to love. Both were right. That calling of God remains our task. Will you hear our calling as we hold no other gods before him?

You shall love the Lord your God with all your heart, and with all your soul, and with all your mind . . . You shall love your neighbor as yourself (Matthew 22:37, 39).

So let us believe in the only God, and so let us love!

Proper 4
Genesis 12:1-9

Blessed To Be A Blessing

Abram was a remarkable man. Forget the fact that he was still able at age 99 to father children! The first remarkable thing about Abram was that he was willing to believe God and so set out on a journey to an unknown land, without the security of country and kindred but only the promise that God would take care of him. How many of you at age 75 or even 35 would make that kind of journey, that kind of commitment?

At first it seems like a rosy future: a great nation, a new land, blessings promised to those whom Abram blesses, and curses on ones whom Abram curses. What could Abram have to lose? Several things come to my mind: a sense of stability, worldly comfort (such as it was in those days), family ties. Gone now were Abram's retirement plans — no 42 parties, no bridge games, no 18 holes of golf three days a week, no playing the stock market with retirement funds, no evening walks in suburbia with Sarai.

Of course, they would get to travel, but that would be without the luxury of American Express and Visa and without the convenience of returning home when they had had enough. Just imagine God going before our adult Sunday school classes and asking for volunteers for this journey! How many couples would be ready to go? Not many, I suppose.

But Abram, despite his age, despite his physical condition, despite the riskiness of pursuing God's promises . . . Abram said "Yes" to God and left for the land of Canaan with only a handful of possessions, a few family members and a bagful of promises from God.

But I wonder if Abram really caught the larger vision. I'm relatively certain that he saw clearly the promise of many blessings: the gift of a great nation, of a new land and of many descendants. But did Abram really grasp the larger picture, the one that most of us really don't see and that even fewer pursue? Did you hear this "master plan" in God's word to Abram? Did you grasp the "purpose" of the Hebrew nation? Did you discover the "overview" of the Old Testament, indeed a key theme of the whole Bible?

This theme is quite obvious. Let me simply read again the verses that contain it. Surely you can pick it out!

> *I will make of you a great nation, and I will bless you, and make your name great, so that you will be a blessing. I will bless those who bless you, and the one who curses you I will curse; and in you all the families of the earth shall be blessed (Genesis 12:2-3 NRSV).*

What is God's overall plan? To make the Hebrews great? To reward the Hebrews for their goodness? To separate out the chosen people in order to honor them, serve them, please them? To play favorites with his children? No!

The purpose behind the blessing of the Hebrews is to bless the world. The role of the Hebrews is not to be favorite sons and daughters but to ensure that all of God's children become truly blessed. To put it simply, Israel was blessed in order to be a blessing. Their primary task in life was not to act as if they were No. 1 but to ensure that even the least of all peoples would feel the showers of God's blessings.

Abram's mission was more than to father an heir or to claim a territory. His mission was to set into motion God's plan of creation, the blessing of every last creature who lives and moves and has being! Now, that is a task worthy of leaving retirement plans behind! That is a task worth the risk! That is a purpose worthy of ultimate commitment!

So it is that the people called Hebrews were given a commission. It was and still is more than survival of a family. It is to be the survival and flourishing of all families. The Jew must concern himself with more than the gift of the land; he also must be concerned with how he may fulfill the call to bless all people — and that means even Palestinians.

But the religious ones called Jews and the citizens called Israelis have no less a biblical commission than we who are Christians and U.S. citizens. The charge that was given to the Hebrews — to bless all people — was taken up by Jesus, for he came to be "a light for revelation to the Gentiles, and for the glory of your people Israel (Luke 2:32)." And that charge was passed on to us, his church: "Go therefore and make disciples of all nations, baptizing them in the name of the Father and of the Son and of the Holy Spirit, and teaching them to obey everything that I have commanded you (Matthew 28:19 NRSV)."

We, no less than the Hebrews, no less than the Jews, are entrusted with blessing our world and its peoples. We are asked to minister to the needy and the vulnerable, not simply to the worthy and the influential.

As a country we are glad to claim God's blessings. We do not totally ignore the many privileges we enjoy. That is not our primary problem. We have no trouble seeing that God has blessed America. Our problem is that we are confused as to why God has blessed us. Many of us think it is because we are great. Many think it is because we have been good. Some even think God has nothing to do with the advantages we enjoy, that they are only the results of our hard work or ingenuity or shrewdness.

Is it possible that whatever blessings God has showered on the United States are not for the sake of our indulgence or a reward for our great behavior but are for a singular purpose, a purpose much the same as that of Abram and his people — that we are blessed in order to be a blessing?

23

Can we now, as a country, move from the role of liberator to that of humanitarian? Can we continue to help the people of Kuwait, so badly brutalized by an oppressive army? And are there not victims also in Iraq, those who were forced into war by terrorism? Can we not have compassion for all of God's people?

I believe that to whatever extent the United States has been blessed, to that extent we are asked to be a blessing. We are not asked by God simply to count our blessings but to share them.

Do you feel resistance inside you when I say, "share?" Would you rather hear the promises of our text to us, the promises of blessings and greatness, and forget the promises made to all of creation?

But our text does not end with a blessing for the Hebrews or his chosen people. It does not stop with a national blessing but reaches its rightful conclusion only with an international blessing.

Today we desperately need a "new world order." By that I do not mean a political structure to maintain peace, as important as that is. What we need is a new world order based on Genesis 12:2-3 where every nation and every religious group sees its mission beyond blessing itself. The new world order will understand that God is not on the side of one nation but of all nations. God does not love some of his people and despise the rest. He has called all of his creation good and chooses to bless it and all its creatures.

Would you be surprised if I told you that Genesis 12 is not just the story of Abram, not just the story of Israelites, not just the story of the Bible, not just an intent of Jesus' ministry, not just a purpose of the church? Would you be shocked if I insisted that Genesis 12 is our story, that it is not simply Abram's purpose but our purpose?

Have we not been blessed in order to be a blessing? If not, then why have we been blessed? Is it because we have been so good? Do you really believe that? Some of our friends may have some doubts about that!

And if we do accept Abram's call, what would that mean? Could we be asked to take some risks, make some sacrifices? Perhaps. Even at age 75? Possibly.

Would more be required of us than simply keeping a running total of our blessings? Yes, more would be required. We would be asked to share, to give.

Would we be expected even with limited talents and resources, to be a blessing? Yes, we would and, yes, we could.

Would we be expected to spend less time and energy blessing ourselves and more time and energy blessing others? Precisely.

"But I want to be blessed." So do others. "But I like my comforts." Can we hear those words, "You are blessed in order to be a blessing?"

"But I am barren. I have no life in me." God promises new life. God empowers us to be blessings. God promises to go with us.

Many centuries ago an old man received a call. Surprisingly, he left his home and ventured out to a new frontier with only the promise of future blessings. He began with a tired, broken-down body, a barren wife, a few possessions. He did not have even a compass to guide him.

But his nation was blessed, and from that nation came a Savior; and from that Savior, a church; and from that church, people committed to continuing Abram's call.

It is a call not to status and favor, not to privilege and honor. It is not a call to amass blessings for ourselves but to be a part of a kingdom where God's master plan unfolds . . . the blessing of all his children.

I have no doubt that we gathered here today are blessed people. I only pray that we will learn to be people who bless others.

That was God's call to Abram.

It is now yours and mine!

Proper 5
Genesis 22:1-18

The Agonizing Provider

Today we look again at Abraham. We remember God's promise of a great nation, a new land and numerous descendants. We remember God's plan to bless all of humanity through him and his people. So we have a right to be thoroughly confused and confounded with the passage before us. Here, in Genesis 22, God asks Abraham to offer his only son as a burnt offering.

And what is even more startling, Abraham responds dutifully and quickly to God's command. Abraham offers no protest, shows no emotion. The story focuses on Abraham's unswerving obedience to God! Abraham does, in fact, all that God asks and apparently is ready to take his own son's life when an angel intervenes. Because of his demonstration of faith, such a sacrifice is not necessary. Abraham has proven his faith in God and his obedience to him.

But there is something obviously missing in our story. I certainly am impressed by Abraham's discipline and obedience, but I would like to see more humanness, more emotion, more inner turmoil. The problem with the way the story is told is that it supplies us only with outward actions. It keeps hidden the inner thoughts and motives of Abraham and reveals nothing of God's concern for the feelings of Isaac or Abraham.

Was this task that God asked of Abraham that perfunctory? Could one easily take the life of one's only son, the son, we are told, that was loved? I am convinced that there is an even deeper drama played out in the heart and mind of Abraham. Surely he struggled with this unbelievable command from God!

How could God dare ask Abraham to give up his only son, the son he loved? How could God ask him to take Isaac as though going on an Indian Guides' campout only then to take his life? How was Abraham able to answer Isaac's questions? How could his heart bear to see the tears in his son's eyes and to hear words of disbelief: "What are you doing? Why are you tying me down? Why, Daddy, why?"

And what about God's promise for descendants? Surely God's promise would die with Isaac! And it would mean that all of Abraham's call had been for nothing — the leaving home at 75, the wanderings, the promises, the great joy of finally having a child.

Surely Abraham struggled with some of these questions! He may have obeyed God without a word on the outside, but from the inside he must have cried out, "My God, my God, why hast thou forsaken me?"

Can you imagine offering your own child or grandchild as a sacrifice to God? I can't. I cannot even relate to cereal offering, burnt offering, animal sacrifice. Human sacrifice is totally foreign to me.

But I do understand the Hebrew notion that we are not to love anything or anybody more than God. I do understand the first commandment. I do remember Jesus' saying that anyone who loved mother or father more than him was not worthy of him. But I still can't imagine God's ever putting us to the test that way, forcing us to choose one or the other.

Keep in mind that in the story a life was never taken. This story does not suggest that God takes children from us if we love them too much. It is a story of Abraham's obedience, not of God's cruel testing. Abraham is quick to point out God's graciousness even after the anguish of his ordeal.

Abraham, once he is delivered from his agonizing call, offers up a name for the place. He calls it "the Lord will provide." Remember that, earlier, Abraham offers the same phrase when Isaac innocently asks him, ". . . where is the lamb for a burnt offering?"

"God will provide . . ."

For our purposes this morning, this phrase is precisely the image of God that I want to suggest — that God is the Great Provider. And more than that, God is at times an agonizing provider.

Of course, there are no signs of God's compassion from the story itself. But one must understand that this God is the same God of the Old Testament who forgives his stubborn people, who has pity on the widow and the fatherless, who accepts scoundrels like Jacob as worthy enough to lead his people. This God of Abraham, Isaac and Jacob is a loving, caring, compassionate, forgiving God. This God also knows judgment, to be sure, but not without a concern for all who suffer.

Let me suggest that if Abraham anguished over the thought of killing his son, if he suffered in the depth of his soul until the final release came from the angel of mercy, if Abraham agonized over his call to obedience, then the God who provided a means of escape agonized with him. God was more than simply a provider; he was a provider linked to the heart and soul of his servant.

I believe the writer of Genesis 22 was primarily interested in showing Abraham's obedience. He gave, therefore, only sketchy details of the experience on the mountain. But I still want to know about Abraham's inner struggles. I am convinced he agonized over what God had asked him to do. If he experienced no agony, then surely this could not have been his only son, the one whom he loved.

But just as I am convinced that Abraham had moments of anguish, I also am concerned that God agonized with him. I am certain that the Great Provider is often the Agonizing Provider, the One who hurts with us and suffers with us.

Our story, of course, has a happy ending. Abraham does not have to kill his only son, the son he loves. When the ordeal is over it is a time for celebration, but not the kind with firecrackers and hurrahs. I imagine instead a tearful embrace of a very emotionally weary old man and a very frightened young lad. Tears would have been more likely than laughter. And in the poignancy of that moment, in the midst of joy spilling out of agony, I am certain that God smiled.

Many victories in life are like that moment. These are victories not without anguish and high cost. When victory comes, it should not be like the frenzy of winning the Super Bowl. Even in the midst of success, the sacrifices cannot be ignored. The pain endured cannot be totally forgotten. Joy is present but it is given shape and character by remaining concern.

Victory in the Persian Gulf was that kind of victory. We could rejoice that our troops came home, that a cruel aggressor had been stopped, that there was an end to intense military conflict, that there was new hope for a lasting peace. But our joy had to be tempered with compassion and concern for those who had suffered and who will continue to suffer, for the needless loss of life, for atrocities to our environment, for destruction of property and livelihood and for the mental anguish of so many people around our globe.

We in America may feel much like Abraham felt at the end of the story. There are indeed sons and daughters we feared we would lose who were spared. For the many lives returned safely to us we are grateful! But our joy is tempered by the knowledge of the many who suffered and died in this conflict. We join with God in compassion for those whose anguish has only begun.

The consequences of this conflict will be borne for decades to come: loss of life, damage to the environment, destruction of property and services. We truly can be grateful for victory, but it is not a victory without agony, it is not a joy undiminished by sorrow. The "stars and stripes" that are waved in victory also cover the coffins of our own who have died.

So where is grace when victory is tainted by agony, when joy has to make room for tears? Abraham believed in the midst of his trial that the Lord would provide, and he knew even after his son was spared that the Lord would continue to provide.

The good news is that the Great Provider is always there — in times of jubilant victory, in times of agonizing defeat and in those rare moments of agonizing victory.

The Great Provider is with us when we leave our security, when we lose our son or daughter, when we face a debilitating illness, when we recover from surgery, when war breaks out, when peace comes.

Saint Francis de Sales once said: "Do not look forward to what might happen tomorrow. The same everlasting Father who cares for you today will take care of you tomorrow and every day. Either he will shield you from suffering, or he will give you unfailing strength to bear it."

In the drama of the crucifixion, we see the story of Abraham revisited. Again we have an only son, a son loved by the Father, a son on whom a promise rests, a son who is in danger. And again it is a story not devoid of agony, anguish and inner wrestling.

But in this greatest of all stories, we are allowed inside the characters. We see the purpose of God for his creation. We know something of the mind of Christ. We witness Christ's agony in the Garden of Gethsemane. And this time the Son is aware of the dangers. He does not look for another sacrifice. If there is to be a sacrifice, he knows it will be his.

But there is a different ending here than in Genesis 22. The hand is not stayed. Death is not prevented. The cup does not pass. And, finally, the ultimate sacrifice is not taken but freely given.

We cannot escape the seriousness of the cross. We cannot deny the agony of the Father, the anguish of the Son. We cannot even hide our own regret for Christ's innocent suffering.

We also have reason to celebrate for we are the recipients of the Christ's blessing. We stand in the presence of Christ, the Agonizing Provider, and we are more grateful than happy. Our joy comes not without tears. Our Easter comes only after Good Friday. Resurrection comes only after the costliness of the cross.

Most of us know of agonizing victories — victories where the price was high. We know of triumph after discipline, sweat and tears. We know of success that sometimes has followed mental anguish, courage and sacrifice.

The God we worship, the God of Abraham, is not a detached God but one acquainted with our grief and with our joys. He is with us in the thrill of victory, the agony of defeat and in that strange experience of victory amidst anguish.

Most of us long for shallow victories. That is, we would be willing to settle for liberation without sacrifice, victory without cost, grace without discipline, resurrection without crucifixion.

And sometimes the hand is stayed and the sacrifice is not made. Sometimes we get well. Sometimes we are reconciled. And in that process toward wholeness, the Great Provider is there.

But other times tragedy knocks on our door, life asks us to pay up, the night comes and the chill shakes our very bones. Isn't it good to know that the Great Provider cares, that our anguish is his anguish and our agony is his agony?

The Provider is always there. Saint Paul tells us, "God is faithful, and he will not let you be tempted beyond your strength, but with the temptation will also provide the way of escape, that you may be able to endure it (1 Corinthians 10:13)."

In our Genesis story, God in his mercy spared Isaac. Abraham was obedient and trusted always that the Lord would provide.

And in our gospel story, God does what he did not ask Abraham to do. He fully offers his only Son, the Son whom he loved, the Son who held promise for all people: "For God so loved the world that he gave his only son, that whoever believes in him should not perish but have everlasting life."

God has always been an agonizing Father. Christ was willing to feel the agony of the cross. And together, Father and Son, they guarantee the call of Abraham to bring a blessing to all people. Indeed, now grace and salvation are available to everyone.

God always has been the Great Provider. He provides for us in the midst of our abundance. He provides for us in the midst of our agony, our time of temptation, our hour of despair. He celebrates with us when our joys triumph over our tears.

So when trials come, when agony appears, when temptation knocks, remember the words of Abraham: "God will provide."

He will indeed!

Birthright Blues

Do you have the "birthright blues?" Jane does. Listen to her story.

Jane: I am so plain and dull that I never have any dates.

Friend: Why don't you go to a good beauty salon and get a different hairdo?

Jane: Yes, but that costs too much money.

Friend: Well, how about buying a magazine with some suggestions for different ways of setting it yourself?

Jane: Yes, I tried that — and my hair is too fine. It doesn't hold a set. If I wear it in a bun, it at least looks neat.

Friend: How about using makeup to dramatize your features, then?

Jane: Yes, but my skin is allergic to makeup. I tried it once and my skin got rough and broke out.

Friend: They have lots of good, non-allergenic makeups out now. Why don't you go see a dermatologist?

Jane: Yes, but I know what he'll say. He'll say I don't eat right. I know I eat too much junk and don't have well-balanced meals. That's the way it is when you live by yourself. Oh, well, beauty is only skin deep.

Friend: Well, that's true. Maybe it would help if you took some adult education courses, like in art or current events. It helps make you a good conversationalist, you know.

Jane: Yes, but they're all at night. And after work I'm so exhausted.

Friend: Well, take some correspondence courses, then.

Jane: Yes, but I don't even have time to write letters to my folks. How could I ever find time for correspondence courses?

Friend: You could find time if it were important enough.

Jane: Yes, but that's easy for you to say. You have so much energy. I'm always so tired.

Friend: Why don't you go to bed at night? No wonder you're tired when you sit up and watch "The Late Show" every night.

Jane: Yes, but I've got to do something fun. That's all there is to do when you're like me![6]

Have you ever met Jane? Have you ever sung her song? Tell me straight: "Do you have the 'birthright blues'?"

In our text for this morning there are many themes worth exploring. One could talk about sibling rivalry, Mama's boy versus Daddy's boy, macho versus cultured, brawn versus brain. But there is one theme that dominates the story and it concerns Esau's birthright. Why did he give it up so easily?

But first let me say a word about the birthright itself. In the Hebrew tradition, a birthright was really the right of the first-born son. It included holding "a position of honor as head of the family and a double share of the inheritance."[7] In this particular case, one would assume it also meant inheriting the promise made to Abraham of a great nation and of a new land.

So this was no small thing that Esau traded away in a matter of minutes — and all for a bowl of lentils! Why did he do so? The easy answer is that he was just stupid. He did not understand the value of the birthright and so he was easily tricked out of it by a cunning younger brother.

One might also assume that Esau was one who lived only for the present moment. To him, "a bird in the hand" was always worth "two in the bush," or in this case, a "bowl in the hand" was surely worth "a birthright in the bush."

Perhaps one could even make the case that Esau was a modernist after all. He must have heard the '60s saying, "If it feels good, do it," and made his own adaptation: "If it looks good, trade for it."

But the last verse of our story suggests that none of these views reflect Esau's primary problem. Verse 34b gives our answer: "Thus Esau despised his birthright." Like our poor little Jane, Esau suffered from the "birthright blues." He did not treasure what he had been given. He was indifferent about it. He would trade it for anything, even the mushy contents of a bowl! To Esau it was worth nothing!

Esau suffered from the "birthright blues," and from that time forward thousands have followed his example. How far will the epidemic spread? It is hard to say. There are so many cases, even today. Are you one of them? Do you hate your birthright?

Do you feel gypped? Do you resent the body you received, your face, your intelligence, your lack of intelligence, your background, your inheritance, your lack of inheritance?

Jesus evidently was aware of the "birthright blues" syndrome. He even dedicated an entire parable to speak to it. You do remember the story about the talents, don't you? The master called his servants together and to one he gave five talents, to another, two, and to another, one. When he returned to receive back the money he had entrusted to them, the ones with two and five talents had used them wisely and doubled their worth, but the one who had only one talent had buried it in the ground.

If you ask me, he had a bad case of the "birthright blues." He was ashamed of what had been given to him. He treated it as if it had little value at all. The master was very angry with this ungrateful servant!

But I have to admit, it is very easy to slip into those "birthright blues." It is very easy to feel sorry for oneself. It is very easy to find others who receive "more" or "better."

So when we stand next to someone with a better body, a better brain, a prettier face, why not succumb to a little "birthright blues?" And why not follow Esau's example? Why not misuse what we have been given? Why not settle for the moment instead of waiting for a future payoff? Why not take something that God gave as special and treat it as though it were worth nothing?

And why should we ever care about the larger picture. Who cares about intended use? Why should we respect our birthright? Are we not free to do with our birthright as we choose? What we have is for our own use or abuse. Am I right?

The ultimate trap is to end up with no birthright at all, feeling that we have no promise from God and nothing to do. So we bury our talent, sell our birthright and join Jane in our pitiful lament: "That's all there is to do when you're like [us]."

But the Bible says otherwise. It tells us to pick up our pallet of self-pity and walk. It tells us to "Go and sin no more." It tells us to welcome the stranger, care for the outcast. It tells us to love our neighbor as ourselves. It tells us to use all that we have for the glory of God, to let our lights shine.

Fortunately, there is an alternative to the "birthright blues." Ask Helen Keller. If anyone could get my vote as the most likely candidate for the "birthright blues," it would be Helen. Born without sight or hearing, she eventually made the journey from self-pity to communication and on to spirituality and love. I challenge any of us to place our self-pity next to hers and feel justified about our moodiness!

Tim Hansel said it right when he wrote, "Pain is inevitable, but misery is optional."[8] The "birthright blues" is a choice. It is not a given!

Perhaps some of you are afraid you will leave the service today without a reverent word. You are not a "plain Jane" or a talent waster. You have no "Cinderella" or "Cinderfella" complex. You do not feel short changed, but rather blessed. So where is your example if not Esau or Jacob?

You might try emulating the servants with the two and five talents by taking what has been given you and using it wisely, not for your own advancement, but for the sake of the Master who entrusted it to you.

The choice we make in life often is between two major options: living as though we have the "birthright blues" or the "birthday bonanza." Most of us feel one way or the other: either basically blessed with what we have been given or basically short changed.

This human dilemma is why this Old Testament lesson is so important to us and so relevant. It asks us if we join Esau in hating our birthright. It asks us if we are willing to settle for the moment, if we treat cheaply what has great value, if we pity ourselves when we have been given much.

So where are you right now? Are you slipping into the "birthright blues?" Are you celebrating your "birthday bonanza?"

And regardless of where you are right now, where do you want to be? Does Esau's route sound okay? Sell out cheap; hate what is yours.

What do you want to do with your talents? Put them alongside others and weep? Put them next to need, and serve?

What will be your basic stance in life? Gratitude or dissatisfaction?

So what will it be for you? Will you cast your pearls before swine, sell your birthright for a cup of chili, bury your talent or use it, be grateful for all that has been given to you or pout in the corner until you win the lottery?

Will you live only for the moment, care more about food and money than meaning and purpose, value life or devalue it?

Let me make it simple for now: What will your autobiography be titled: *Birthright Blues* or *Birthday Bonanza?* You decide!

Stairways Of Heaven

As I studied in depth this passage of scripture, I learned that I have long carried misconceptions about "Jacob's ladder." My first surprising discovery was that all the commentaries I read suggested that Jacob's vision was not of a ladder as we know it today, but more of a "ramp" or "stair-like pavement."[9] This "ramp" was to handle traffic between heaven and earth.[10] Heavenly messengers could approach thereby those dwelling below.

After reading about Jacob's ladder being a ramp-like structure, I decided to look at the familiar song I loved to sing at youth camp, "We Are Climbing Jacob's Ladder." We would sing the song as we walked in single file up the path at night to the outdoor chapel. But when I studied the song's text, I soon realized that it really was not about the story of Jacob found in Genesis, but simply used its imagery.

Jacob's story is not about Jacob or any human creature's climbing "higher and higher." It is not about our moving toward God. Jacob's story is about God's coming lower and lower, closer and closer, that he might be near and dear to us. Jacob's story is not about a holy man going to a holy place to meet God. It is about a fugitive, scared of a brother's wrath, who is encountered by the God of his fathers, the God of Abraham and Isaac.

Do you remember what has happened just before Jacob's dream? Jacob has tricked his father into giving him the blessing rather than to his brother, Esau, and once his trickery has been discovered, decides it's healthier to find a new residence — pronto! In other words, the hairy-chested brother, Esau, has discovered that he has been betrayed and apparently is ready to eliminate his sibling rival forever.

So when Jacob lies down to take his rest, it is not after he has attended vespers or said his prayers — except maybe prayers for protection. Jacob is little more than a fugitive on the run, stopping to get enough sleep to continue his journey. Jacob pauses for sleep, but what he receives will be far more refreshing, far more empowering, far more advantageous than a restful slumber. He receives an encounter with God: a vision of a ladder or "ramp" and a speech from God that renews his promise to Abraham's descendants.

I have uneasy feelings as I envision the image of the "ramp." It brings to mind escalators, which have not turned out to be my best friends. I sincerely hope that heaven does not have an escalator as a means of entry. If so, I may never be able to enter. Let me explain.

When I am at a mall, I invariably go to the wrong place to catch the escalator. If I want to go up I make my way past cosmetics and the men's department and finally arrive at the escalator entrance. Of course, when I make it to the entrance, the steps are going down, not up. And, as you might have guessed, the up escalator is on the other side of the store, past ladies' lingerie and housewares.

This has happened to me so many times that I have become suspicious the escalators are engineered so that they can be rotated half a turn and that someone, who hates either ministers or people with last names like mine, stand at the controls. If I start in the right direction toward the right escalator, he rotates the escalator away from me. If I start out wrong, he allows me the privilege of messing up by myself.

The fact is that there never seems to be an escalator going in the right direction. Or, to put that same idea theologically, there does not seem to be a way to go up when I'm feeling down. There does not seem to be an access to heaven when the world has dropped me in the pit.

But our story of Jacob would disagree with that conclusion. It would insist that heaven and earth are conveniently connected. Even better, it would insist that the God on high is willing and able to come down to us, even when we least expect him, in places both holy and secular, at times when we are saints and more often when we are sinners, at times of the "blues" and the "blahs."

The story of Jacob's ladder is not about a sweet encounter in the "Garden of Prayer." It is about the Creator of heaven and earth finding a fugitive in flight and giving him a large dose of grace, an ample portion of promise, a full anointing of his Spirit. It is about God providing an escalator when we need it the most.

When God comes down to speak with Jacob it is not through a burning bush. He speaks to him in a dream. Of course, dreams always have been a means by which God could speak. Dreams also are ways for us to become aware of our innermost selves or our anxieties and fears. In our story, God does speak to Jacob through a dream and the message is clear. The ramp or ladder becomes an important image as it reminds us of God's accessibility to us. Jacob discovered that even away from his homeland, he was not alone. He discovered that even in his sinfulness, God approached him. Now he knew that heaven and earth could touch in unexpected times and places. The God on high was not content to keep his heavenly distance.

And God also makes sure that Jacob hears again the promise first made to Abraham, a promise of a land and of many descendants. But the main message, I believe, is one that relates to the image of a ladder, or what we may refer to as the ramp or staircase or even "gate of heaven" that Jacob uses at the end of the story. In verse 15, God gives a fanfare to his message with the word "Behold." The good news follows: "Behold, I am with you and will keep you wherever you go . . . ."

That's a nice dream, don't you think? Wouldn't you like a dream like that to replace some of the weird ones you have? It is a good dream to dream anytime, but what a special dream for Jacob at that time and place. With a stone for a pillow and hard ground for a bed, with fear surging through his body and anxiety running rampant in his mind, Jacob found not a wrestling opponent but the Prince of Peace to calm his fears. Jacob received words of grace from God: "I will be with you;" you are not alone.

Perhaps we need today a new Christian symbol: an ancient, dirt-paved ramp or perhaps a modern escalator. Both would point to the good news: There is not just one access to God and heaven. The "up" ramp for us and the "down" ramp for God always are side by side. The gateway of heaven is not hidden behind the hardware department. It is not obscured by the walls of fear or the darkness of tragedy, or blocked by the stockpiles of our sin.

The good news is that God's escalators are everywhere. The stairways of heaven are no farther than the breath of God's Spirit or the sigh of our prayers. Heaven and earth are forever connected. Why? Not because we always choose to go up to him, but because God never fails to come down to us. There is an escalator by every pit we ourselves dig and by every pit provided by life. God's promise to Jacob is given to us as well: "I will be with you." And Jesus repeats that promise: ". . . and lo I am with you always, to the close of the age."

The modern symbol of the escalator reminds us of the good news: Even in exile, our God descends to us. The gateways of heaven are always open. The stairways from heaven to earth are always available to two-way traffic. We can go up; God can come down. We can seek our Father; the Great Shepherd can and does seek us. We can take Jacob's ladder and climb higher, higher. But we must never forget how it all started. God has always come lower, lower, before we have been able to go higher, higher. Remember, the tower of Babel failed. We, by ourselves, cannot reach God or become like God. Earth cannot reach heaven until heaven comes to us.

In the movie, *Field of Dreams*, only dreamers saw the vision. Only those touched by heaven could understand. Those who live only in the realm of earth — who never realize the heavenly visits, who never hear heavenly voices — may well remain hopeless skeptics.

But Jacob caught the vision. He caught it not simply because he saw a ladder or ramp. He caught it because he accepted the promises God gave to him and, as he did, heaven and earth touched. The good news that claimed him made earth and stone a holy place.

But did you hear Jacob's confession? The verse that stands out for me is this: "Surely the Lord was in this place and I did not know it." Does that fit your experience? Have you ever been in God's presence and hardly noticed it? Have you ever suddenly realized that God had been with you long before you knew he was there? Have you ever been in exile or in fear only to discover the Spirit of God coming to your aid?

The good news of Jacob's story is not simply that there are links to heaven. The good news is not that God sometimes comes to us. The good news is not that heaven and earth are somehow connected, making encounters possible. The good news is all but hidden in the sentence, "Surely the Lord was in this place, and I did not know it." Do you understand? Do you have it?

The promise of God is not what will be or can be; the promise concerns what is! God is with us! God is with us in our exile and in our pain, in our fears and in our joys, in our sin and in our service, in our homeland and in our new frontiers. The good news is this: God is with us always — whether we know it or not!

On the way to one of our favorite spots — Cuchara, Colorado — there is a formation that has been named the "Giant Staircase." It is a huge mass of stone that forms three or four gigantic steps. After studying this text I would like to rename those steps the "Staircase of Heaven." I did not name it the staircase *to* heaven because we are not giants who unassisted can make our way to heaven. It is God on high who

45

brings a touch of heaven to us. The stairs originate not on earth but in heaven. It is the God who promises to be with us who connects forever heaven and earth.

The good news is that there are staircases of heaven all around us. There are spiritual escalators everywhere. These escalators have the "up" and "down" ramps side by side for easy access. We may approach God. God will meet us. And God will meet us in the strangest of places. He greets us at the tomb. He encounters us at the cross. He meets us at the graveside of our grief. The "visitor of dreams" comes to us in our sleeping and in our waking. He comes to us so often when we are unaware.

The One who comes down to us invites us to rise and walk. He invites us to rise and live again. The One who meets us promises to be with us forever and wherever. So the next time we are on the run, the next time fear has the best of us, the next time we are estranged from a brother or sister, the next time we feel lost in a foreign land, let us remember Jacob's dream and the promise of God's presence.

We should not be surprised to find God there. We know to look for escalators in the strangest of places. Heaven and earth meet not once but many times. So on our journey, as we fall into the pit or as we climb higher and higher to get a glimpse of God, we should not be surprised to discover that "Behold, the God of Jacob . . . is already with us!"

Proper 8
Genesis 32:22-32
Hip Pointer

Our narrative begins with Jacob's sending his family across the Jabbok stream while staying behind to spend the night alone. Tomorrow he must face his brother, Esau, whom he has not seen since he escaped after stealing Esau's blessing and having fleeced him out of his birthright. Jacob does not know how his brother will receive him . . . but several possibilities have occurred to him — none of them positive.

It should come as no surprise that Jacob got little sleep that night. Who could sleep well, knowing that one must stand in front of an angry brother and beg for forgiveness?

The story of Jacob's wrestling is one of the most widely discussed passages of all the patriarch material.[11] This is partially due to the fact that this is a complex and somewhat confusing story. For example, how many of you can name Jacob's adversary? Did Jacob wrestle all night with a man, an angel, God, or a combination of all of these? The text leaves all of these as possibilities.

At one point there is a reference to a man and, at another, God and man. Later in the story this enemy does not have enough power to quickly defeat Jacob yet has enough power to bestow a blessing. So is he, or it, human or divine?

Perhaps the ambiguity, the mystery, makes the story even more relevant to us. Many of our enemies have no clear identity: an illness with no name and no cure, a depression that won't leave us, a sluggish economy that results in the loss of a job. It is not easy for us to fight an enemy we cannot clearly identify. We are often left with only the veiled enemies we call fate, or fear, or self-doubt, or guilt. These mysterious enemies are difficult to defeat! So in this story perhaps it is not important to know the identity of Jacob's sparring partner. The more important thing is discerning Jacob's strategy for victory.

Central to the story is the fact that Jacob was victorious neither by virtue of his being fearless (indeed he was quite frightened — both of Esau and of this stranger) nor by reason of his super-human strength (for he never really defeated his enemy outright). Rather, Jacob received a reward because he was tenacious and hopeful; he would not quit until he got a blessing.

But, even so, the story suggests the presence of grace. That is to say, Jacob does not force his enemy or God to give him a blessing. Rather, it seems that God in his mercy awards him a gift after struggle: Jacob no longer will be called Jacob but will have a new identity. He no longer will be Jacob ("heel/ trickster/over-reacher . . .") but Israel, which may mean "God Rules, God Preserves, God Protects . . . ."[12] Out of Jacob's struggle, the chosen people called Israelites are born.

If we, like Jacob, receive a blessing through struggle, the credit belongs both to God and to us. But we should never forget that the very possibility for a blessing is a gift from God, a legacy left for each one of us.

There is one other point of the story that I would like to emphasize: Though there was a blessing for Jacob, it came only after a long and difficult struggle. The encounter ended not with a "happily ever after" finish but with Jacob's walking away with a pronounced limp. So, to say that every struggle has a blessing does not mean there is no price to pay. To say that every cloud has a silver lining does not mean we are prevented from getting drenched or even spared from catching the flu. The plot of Jacob's encounter does not read like a fairy tale. Everything does not change with the wave of a magic wand but only after sweat and struggle. Jacob's story is a true-to-life story: Somewhere in the midst of an almost overwhelming struggle there can be significant gain. At times the gain may even justify the suffering. If not, it is still worthy of effort.

I believe that Jacob's struggle has many parallels to our own battles and that his rewards can be our rewards. The biblical faith as a whole and ordinary life in particular both bear out the fact that human struggle always has within it the potential for gain — always!

First, let me offer a very personal example. In December of last year I developed what was first diagnosed as a sciatic-nerve problem. I had to stand through every church service in late December. In January the doctors discovered a damaged disc and I had to have back surgery. The whole experience was both traumatic and enriching. This particular passage now has special meaning to me. I can identify with Jacob's wrestling and his ailment.

It was amusing to me that, as I read one of the commentaries, there was a reference not to the "sinew of the hip" but to one particular nerve of the hip and leg — a part of the anatomy that has become very familiar to me: the "sciatic nerve."[13]

During this past year I have struggled not only with this sciatic nerve but also with such things as fear, anxiety, discomfort, pain, boredom. But through this experience I also am very conscious of many blessings.

The most obvious blessing was a new awareness and compassion for what so many others have weathered before me — the vulnerability of experiencing an illness that could not be quickly diagnosed or quickly treated, the uncertainty of surgery, the psychological and mental anguish of taking an M.R.I. test while being claustrophobic. Through these many experiences and feelings, I gained a new sensitivity to the plight of others, a new fervor for prayer and a renewed compassion I hope I will never lose.

The second blessing was a most pleasant reward. I received something in my struggle that Jacob was denied: the gift of loving support and encouragement in the midst of my struggle. Jacob was all alone when he met his nocturnal enemy; I had the thoughts and prayers of many. I had cards and phone calls to cheer me and urge my recovery. I am now convinced more than ever of the importance of letting others know that we care when they are going through sickness, surgery or crisis.

This morning I want to share with you a glimpse of some of that encouragement. It began with notes and cards that expressed one key theme: "Our thoughts and prayers are with you." Doesn't it make a difference when we hear those words in our time of trial?

I received a tape from the kindergarten and 3- and 4-year-old classes. What a joy to listen to their voices!

I received many warm and colorful greetings:

"Cheer up, 'cause God loves you! . . . And any friend of God's is a friend of mine!"

"Heard you had an operation! . . . Hope it didn't take too much out of you!"

"Hear you're in the hospital! . . . What some people won't do for a little attention!"

But one card was especially appropriate. A woman who had suffered for many months with an injury, sent me not a get-well card but a sympathy card. She wanted me to know that she knew how I felt!

To help me with my personal struggle, I received a lot of cards with advice:

"Don't let your doctor put one of those sticks in your mouth . . . until you know who ate the ice cream."

"Please take good care of yourself . . . I have enough to worry about without adding you to my list."

As you can see, I had many words of encouragement. These cards and notes were a blessing in and of themselves. But the feeling of being loved and appreciated — that was a great gift!

Most of you have had your share of struggles. Many of them, I'm sure, had blessings that came with them — especially if you kept struggling, kept hoping, kept expecting that there would be a payoff somewhere. Why, indeed, should we ever suffer pain without staying around long enough to receive our blessing? There always is one there. Do you believe that?

Paul believed that. My grandmother believed that. Dr. Albert Outler, noted theologian, believed that. Some of your closest friends, ones who have suffered much, believe that. No matter what the struggle, no matter who the enemy, no matter how terribly long the battle, there is a blessing to be received.

Struggle with guilt? There is forgiveness and hope. Struggle with fear? There is peace of mind in the future. Wrestle with illness? There is strength sufficient for the hour. Out of work? There is a new perspective to be gained. Concerned for a loved one? There is a faith that offers abiding presence for them and for us. Struggling with a relationship? There is the possibility for reconciliation or, if not, the gift of the power and presence of God.

There is no personal struggle for which there is no blessing. That does not mean there will be no pain or no need for courageous endurance. That does not mean we will walk away with no scars or with no limp. But it does mean that human struggle has a purpose, that struggling is not for naught, that life is never hopeless.

What would have happened if Jacob had yelled "Uncle?" What if he had "thrown in the towel" before daybreak? Would God have been forced to go to "Plan B?"

We don't know what would have happened had Jacob given up, but we do know about ourselves. We all know times when we have stopped short in our struggle, when we've had our fill of struggling and quit before the payoff. We all know the empty feeling that comes when we have experienced the pain without receiving the payoff. But that is as tragic as going through a domestic fight, getting all upset and never having the joy of making up! Jacob's strategy, Jacob's advice, makes good sense: "Don't let go until the blessing!"

I must admit that there are times when Jacob's principle is put to the ultimate test. There are times when we are ill and we do not return to health. There are times when personal relationships end in betrayal. There are times when the enemy we are fighting is so strong and so persistent that there seems little chance for victory or for blessing.

But I am claiming that every difficult struggle has not just a "token" blessing, but a significant one, that clouds have more than just a pretty silver lining — that they are draped with the rainbows of God's blessing.

I'm not talking about "success theology" preached on television. I am not promising you as Christians a better job, restored health, material abundance or a life without tragedy. I'm talking about the promise of blessing in every struggle.

I'm not talking about a consolation prize as in the story of the Kansas farmer who had fat chickens because they fed on the swarms of grasshoppers that had stripped bare his crops and pasture. I'm not talking about a magic wand that removes the struggles of life, or takes away all scars, or ensures that there will be no limp, no residual signs of our struggle. Don't we as Christians have the cross as our symbol of faith? Don't we proclaim victory in the midst of defeat? Do we not believe in the resurrection of the dead?

I'm talking today about a faith in God in the midst of every struggle, a faith that will see us through the daily battle with alcohol, or the lifelong struggle for self-worth, or the constant battle with poor health. I'm talking about believing that one can find blessings in the strangest of places. And we find them in part because we hang in, hold on, hang tough.

But more important, we find blessings in every struggle because God puts them there. He hides these treasures in the tall grass of adversity and hopes we will search long and hard enough to find them.

One of my favorite cantatas by Alice Parker is "Melodious Accord." It ends with a magnificent hymn titled "God Moves in a Mysterious Way." Two verses proclaim the central message of Jacob's hopeful endurance:

> *Ye fearful saints, fresh courage take;*
> *The clouds ye so much dread*

Are big with mercy, and shall break in blessings on
    your head.
Judge not the Lord by feeble sense,
But trust him for his grace;
Behind a frowning providence he hides a smiling face.[14]

Jacob was right. He believed there was a blessing some-where in his struggle. He wrestled even in the midst of his fear. He dared to ask for that which he did not deserve. He endured and received a new identity and a new direction.

Saint Paul would endorse Jacob's belief that there is bless-ing in every struggle. But Paul's affirmation would be based not only on the human struggle, but also on Paul's experience of the risen Christ.

Paul believed that every traumatic struggle in life had a blessing. For Paul, that blessing, that guarantee, that ultimate reality was there in the face of any enemy, any danger, any hardship, any challenge. Paul specifically named that ultimate blessing in his letter to the church at Rome:

What then shall we say to this? If God is for us, who is against us? . . . Who shall separate us from the love of Christ? Shall tribulation, or distress, or persecution, or famine, or nakedness, or peril, or sword? . . . No, in all these things we are more than conquerors through him who loved us. For I am sure that neither death, nor life, nor angels, nor principalities, nor things present, nor things to come, nor powers, nor height, nor depth, nor anything else in all creation, will be able to separate us from the love of God in Christ Jesus our Lord (Romans 8:31, 35, 37-39).

As we struggle with life, we need not quit. We have the presence and power of God to see us through. So hang in, hold on, hang tough. A blessing is on its way!

Perfect Strangers

Today we leave the book of Genesis to begin the saga of Exodus. First we examine two stories: one about the plight of the Hebrew people following the death of Joseph and the other concerning the birth of Moses. Both are about strangers. One story entails slavery and suffering, the other compassion and adoption. One is about "imperfect strangers" who remain such. The other is about complete strangers who become very close as adopted child and mother.

Story number one sets the scene with one short verse: "Now there arose a new king over Egypt who did not know Joseph (Exodus 1:8)." Once the rulers of Egypt lost their memory of Joseph and the great things he had done for Egypt, they had little affection for the Hebrews. Indeed, they began to fear them. Ironically, they feared them because of their great numbers, which was part of God's promise to Abraham of numerous descendants.

Driven by fear, the Egyptians enslaved the Hebrews and made them work long and hard. But the Hebrews increased in number all the more. Finally, the Pharaoh took drastic steps to curtail these outsiders: He decreed that all of the male children of the Hebrews be thrown into the Nile. With such violence, our first story of suffering ends and the backdrop for our next story is lowered into place.

Our second story has a more joyous ending — that of providence and mercy. But it begins as the other story ended — with suffering and danger. In this story the babe Moses is placed in a basket, and set adrift on the Nile River in hopes of sparing his life. So it is that two strangers meet, the Pharaoh's daughter and a tiny Hebrew infant who wins her heart and engages her compassion. Though the daughter of Pharaoh knows this is a male Hebrew child, she arranges for his care. Moses is saved by the bell — a b-e-l-l-e, that is. Moses' mother gains the unlikely position of being paid to nurse her own child.

In this second story, compassion and mercy have defeated self-interest and fear. The hard heart of the father is supplanted by the compassion of the daughter. Complete strangers become "perfect" strangers as mother and daughter. Instead of the tiny stranger being sentenced to suffering or death, he will be given a life of privilege in the Pharaoh's house.

These two stories have great relevance to us today. We can identify with many of the various aspects of the story. No matter how many friends we now have, no matter how socially secure we feel, we still have not forgotten what it feels like to be the stranger. Am I right?

Do you remember how you felt in a new school, a new neighborhood, a strange city, a foreign country? Do you remember how it feels to be a stranger before discovering that first friend or receiving that first act of human warmth or kindness?

I can tell you that the feeling of being included is a much better feeling than that of being a stranger! Surely you agree!

We all know the pain of being the stranger. But we also know how it feels to be the people of Egypt and to be threatened by the presence of strangers, especially when their numbers are great.

There are those in Texas who have fear that strangers from the south, the illegal aliens from Mexico, will create real problems for Texas: problems of education, taxes, crime, job markets and medical care. These are not imagined fears. They have grounding in situations we now are facing in our schools, hospitals, marketplace and neighborhood communities.

Like the Egyptians and their rulers, we may have concern for the impact of strangers in our midst. We do not have to be heartless to believe that their presence may prove costly to us. But sometimes these strangers have real faces. It is then that our hearts and our minds do not always agree. It is then that our prejudices and self-interests may be challenged.

Not long ago we used the services of a young Hispanic housekeeper named Patricia. She came to our home for several hours each Thursday. Not long after she began working for us she told me her story. Her recent life history becomes even more dramatic when one parallels it with the story of Moses.

Patricia came from Mexico. There her family was forced into hard labor. They were not slaves of a ruler; they simply were captive to a feeble economy and a very low standard of living. To escape the plight of their environment and to provide for the safety of their family, Patricia and her husband decided to hide in the "bulrushes" of the Rio Grande. They decided to seek safe harbor in the land of the United States. But in their first attempt, they failed. They were caught and sent back.

On their second attempt, Patricia was pregnant with their first child. She could not swim so she had to be pulled across the river on an inner tube. This time she and her husband made it to safety, or at least relative safety. For the next several years she and her family lived in constant fear of being discovered. Finally, they were granted amnesty and citizenship. Recently, Patricia received another level of new freedom and privilege — a Texas driver's license!

One who once was stranger to us now is officially a part of us. Patricia may not be a native Texan but she is at least a native living in Texas. Unlike Moses she was not saved by an individual act of compassion. You might say it was Pharaoh himself who saved her — "Uncle Sam" as we call him. It was our government who offered her an extended hand. She was formally adopted by our nation and our state. Now she has a chance for more than basic survival. Patricia did not fare as well as baby Moses. She was not taken to a palace but only given a greater chance to improve the living conditions of her family.

Like the Egyptians and their rulers in the biblical story, there are Americans and Texans who have fears and concerns about these "strangers" who cross our borders. And I concede that these fears have some substance to them. But for today I celebrate for this one who once was a stranger. I am glad for her. I am glad that the bulrushes were high enough and that my "Uncle Sam" was gracious enough. I am glad that Patricia and her family have found a new life across the border.

I realize that the issues concerning illegal aliens are very complex. I realize that strangers can and do pose an economic threat to people of a country or state. But I also know this personally: Patricia cannot be a stranger to me any longer. For her I want a good life. For her and her family I want a chance for survival. I observe her hard work. I sense her good character. I welcome her now as a friend.

The motives of the Pharaoh are understandable but they are not commendable. The concern of the Egyptians for their own well-being was legitimate but not at the expense of the Hebrews. The fear of the stranger, you see, may be based on real data, but the welcoming of the stranger is based on the true gospel.

As a Christian I am called to reject the action of the Pharaoh who acted out of self-interest and fear and to follow the example of Pharaoh's daughter who acted out of compassion for the stranger. I am not permitted to be an imperfect stranger. To the outsider I am asked to be a perfect stranger!

When I was in high school, a young student came from Germany to be a foreign exchange student in our high school. I did not know him or feel very comfortable around him at first. I invited him to a basketball game and to my house for a visit and we soon became friends. Why did I invite him? I think my parents suggested it — but so did my religion and so did my conscience. I did not think it was fair for him to be a stranger among us and have no one to welcome him.

What a delight when, two summers ago, our whole family went as strangers to Germany. But we did not have to tour as complete strangers. A family outside of Nuremberg welcomed us warmly. They welcomed us into their own home, they fed us and entertained us. The stranger that I had welcomed 28 years before became the friend who welcomed me and my family to a foreign land!

Being the stranger is no fun at all! Becoming the friend of a stranger is often a delight! As Christians we are called to be "perfect strangers," people who welcome those who would stand alone without our support. And could it be that we are called to welcome even the stranger who lowers our economy or our standard of living — even strangers who come in great numbers, even those who heighten our anxiety or fears?

Today we live among many strangers. And if you are like me, you are less in the habit of welcoming the stranger now than you once were. There was a time when I would not pass a moving van on my street without stopping. But now movers come and go and I not only fail to greet the new family moving in; at times I have failed to be acquainted with the family who is moving out.

How about you? Do you welcome the stranger? Do you watch along the shores of your River Nile for signs of endangered strangers, strangers with special needs? Do you welcome the visitor, invite into your home the neighbor, speak to the new resident on your block, ask the new associate at work to join you for church?

We are more than our neighbor's keeper. We are the welcoming committee for the stranger. We are the ones who are to help someone find a sense of belonging.

Maybe our problem is that we have gotten too busy or have become satisfied with the friends we have. Or maybe we think we don't need to be a friend; we already have friends.

But we of the church are called to be "perfect strangers," to welcome those we don't know and to continue to nurture those we do know. Why be perfect strangers? Because no one wants to stay a stranger forever. Everyone wants to belong. We can help make that experience possible.

Some of the words to the theme song of "Cheers" make more sense as a description of a church than of a neighborhood bar: ". . . where everybody knows your name, where everyone's glad you came" — in other words, where no one is a stranger!

In our church and in our city strangers come every week. Some have crossed the border, some have crossed the Mason-Dixon line, some have come from another country, another culture. Some will seem a threat to us, some will be delightful to us. Some will be different. Some will share our background and ideals. But if we follow our Christian calling and welcome them all, then we have the possibility of becoming one people and being strangers no more. Never again will we be nobodies. Never again will we be imperfect strangers. Never again will we be totally alone. We now share a common identity, a common citizenship, a high privilege together. 1 Peter can then be our motto and our song:

> But you are a chosen race, a royal priesthood, a holy nation, God's own people, that you may declare the wonderful deeds of him who called you out of darkness into his marvelous light. Once you were no people but now you are God's people; once you had not received mercy but now you have received mercy (1 Peter 2:9-10).

Now we are not strangers to God or to one another. We are God's people and sisters and brothers together. But strangers come to our door. Strangers still come to our church. Strangers still come to our neighborhood and city.

Pharaoh has his job and we have ours. What will we seek: protection from strangers or the strangers themselves? Do not even be surprised if the stranger you welcome has an accent that betrays him; I believe he's from Galilee.

Water Boy

Today's scripture provides for many sermon possibilities. I could have dealt with Moses' swift departure from Egypt and preached about running from our foes and our fears. I could have taken the second half of our story and played with the notion that here shepherds are not the honored guests of the Christ child but bullies who mistreat all seven of Reuel's daughters. And a most tempting choice would have been to speak of the "spoils of hospitality." Just for defending women's rights, Moses is presented with a prize — nothing less than one of Reuel's daughters, Zipporah. I can assure you, however, that it will take much more than providing water for my herds for me to give away in marriage my daughter, Alison, especially to a total stranger!

Instead of the many preaching possibilities, I have chosen to concentrate on only one verse, verse 17, where Moses takes his stand on behalf of Reuel's daughters: "The shepherds came and drove them away; but Moses stood and helped them, and watered their flock."

In this one act, Moses came into full social consciousness; he changed from fugitive to hero. He first sought to save his own life by leaving Egypt; here in Midian he sought to save the women from their plight.

61

Moses' status is one that changes many times: from Hebrew baby in danger to privileged prodigy of Pharaoh's court, from defender of Hebrew rights to fugitive from justice, from foreigner in flight to protector of the oppressed.

But it is at the Midian watering hole that Moses "comes of age." There he stood up for the daughters of Reuel and made the shepherds back down. There he found new courage and a new sense of social justice. This was a justice based not on color or creed but on the sacred rights of the individual.

What exactly happened at the watering hole? The women probably had gone through the painstaking task of letting down skin pails to deep springs below and then filling the drinking troughs. Then the shepherds arrived and decided to use the women's water for their own herds.[15] Moses interceded on the women's behalf and made the shepherds leave the water for the women and their flock. Without his aid, the women would have had to wait for the shepherds to water their herds, redraw more water and then give drink to their livestock. Moses' intervention saved them time and ensured them of receiving water from a limited and scarce supply.[16]

Moses had fought for Hebrews' rights in Egypt over the issue of cruel treatment. Here in a foreign land he defended the "water rights" of these women. Water was a valuable and scarce commodity — precious!

Water once was a precious commodity to me and "water rights" a very important issue. When I was part of the Crossett High football team and those terrible August practices — "two-a-days" we called them — water was a very precious commodity. After practicing on the distant practice field, we would have to walk past a 12-inch water main that was about one foot above ground and, wouldn't you know it, it had a convenient leak exactly where we crossed it. Precious water squirted four feet in the air — cool, clear water!

But like the women of Midian we were cruelly denied "water rights" by the stately shepherds of our team. (Back in the "Dark Ages" coaches thought that drinking water was bad for one's health and would "undo" all the good of a 100-degree workout.)

I know from personal experience that water can be precious. I understand the pain of seeing water only to have someone bigger deny access to it.

But if we are to look for parallel issues for today, we might look beyond water rights. What are the precious commodities of today to which some people are denied access? What are some of the limited resources that must be distributed with some sense of justice? And who will ensure that the weak or the oppressed will be able to receive their share?

Our state is now trying to solve the problem of both limited funds and the need for improved education. The issue is one involving justice. How does one ensure quality education for all including the disadvantaged? How do we provide adequate education for those who will experience little quality education at home and who already are disadvantaged?

Another issue in our country and state is affordable housing. How can we make housing possible for those willing to train and work and save? Who will stand and defend their rights? Who will join the cause of such groups as "Habitat for Humanity" or "Common Ground" to see that a place to live is within the reach of all?

There are so many issues for social justice and basic human needs. There are ample opportunities to be advocates for fairness and justice in the areas of hunger, education and job opportunity. If we are to play the part of advocate and helper, we first will have to learn to see the need and feel the injustice. We will have to have greater compassion than we have right now for the lesser ones of our society.

One of my favorite quotes from Albert Schweitzer comes from his book, *Out of My Life and Thought*. He shares an experience from one of his many trips.

> *At the station at Tarascon we had to wait for our train in a distant goods shed. My wife and I, heavily laden with baggage, could hardly get along over the shingle between the lines. Thereupon a poor cripple whom I had treated in the camp came forward to help us. He had no baggage*

*because he possessed nothing, and I was much moved by
his offer, which I accepted. While we walked along side
by side in the scorching sun, I vowed to myself that in
memory of him I would in the future always keep a look-
out at stations for heavily laden people, and help them.*[17]

An eye for the overburdened — do we have it? An eye for
injustice — can we see it? Compassion for the weaker ones
— is it alive within us? Or have we grown cold and indifferent — satisfied with our own place of privilege?

We can respond in many ways. We can support local food
banks, housing projects. We can become involved in tutoring
projects. And we can keep an eye out at all the train stations
and all the watering holes to see that people in need are not
forgotten.

There are many people in our society who suffer much more
than these daughters of Reuel. There are many who have lost
hope, many who are defenseless and vulnerable, many who
are hungry, many who are homeless, many who are trapped
in the world of drugs and crime and wretched living conditions.

And if we are to take Moses' act of courage not as the sole
role of a prophet but as the calling of every Christian, then
we must be willing to take on a new and heavy responsibility.
It is my strong conviction that we are called to do much more
than offer the cup of cold water; we also may have to defend
the rights of those at the watering hole. We may have to be
more than angels of mercy; we may have to be angels of justice.

I am convinced that Moses' act at the watering hole at Midian was not the isolated act of a prophet but a model for our
involvement in human history. Jesus gives further witness that
compassion should lead us into ministry and injustice spur us
into action. Consider Jesus' compassion for the outcast lepers,
his ministry to the Samaritan woman at the well, his defense
of the woman guilty of adultery, his driving the money changers
out of the temple.

But whether we are angels of mercy or advocates of justice,
our stance is not one of arrogance or pride but that of humility.

If we are to serve our world as Christians, if we are to defend the weak, it is justice we seek, not limelight.

Ruth Calkin gives us cause to ponder our motives and the proper posture for our service. She writes:

"I Wonder"
You know, Lord, how I serve you
with great emotional fervor
In the limelight.
You know how eagerly I speak for you
At a women's club.
You know how I effervesce when I promote
A fellowship group.
You know my genuine enthusiasm
At a Bible study.

But how would I react, I wonder
if you pointed to a basin of water
And asked me to wash the calloused feet
Of a bent and wrinkled old woman
Day after day
Month after month
In a room where nobody saw
And nobody knew.[18]

Today I believe we are asked to take on new ventures. We still are asked to offer the cup of cold water to the thirsty. But we also are called to care about justice issues, about the distribution of such precious commodities as education, job opportunity, medical care, housing and food.

We must be willing to be advocates without reward. We must be willing to get our hands dirty. We must be willing to stoop and we must not expect in return either hospitality or the gift of a daughter.

Moses has given us an example. Jesus has called us into servant ministry. Concern for justice makes of us advocates when we would rather be bystanders. Eyes that see human hurt ask that we play the part of servant, not master. And through it all we realize that justice knows no race or creed. We all are part of God's family. We all should have access to the watering hole. We all have needs that generate compassion.

A hymn in our new United Methodist hymnal points us in the right direction. It offers the posture of a servant and the compassion of a caring follower of Christ. Will you hear it again and afresh?

> *Jesu, Jesu, fill us with your love,*
> *show us how to serve*
> *the neighbors we have from you,*
>
> *Kneels at the feet of his friends,*
> *silently washes their feet.*
> *Master who acts as a slave to them.*
>
> *Jesu, Jesu, fill us with your love,*
> *show us how to serve*
> *the neighbors we have from you.*
>
> *Neighbors are rich and poor,*
> *neighbors are black and white,*
> *neighbors are near and far away.*
>
> *Jesu, Jesu, fill us with your love,*
> *show us how to serve*
> *the neighbors we have from you.*
>
> *Loving puts us on our knees,*
> *serving as though we are slaves,*
> *this is the way we should live with you.*
>
> *Jesu, Jesu, fill us with your love,*
> *show us how to serve*
> *the neighbors we have from you.*[19]

The Burning Bush Within Us

The flame is a part of our biblical heritage, from the burning bush, to pillars of fire, to the flaming tongues of the Spirit at Pentecost.

The flame is a part of our church tradition and biblical tradition. It symbolizes the Spirit of God that interacts with us in so many different ways. Today we take a look at Moses' experience at the burning bush. From this account we may learn many things about ourselves and about the God we worship.

Several years ago, Dr. Bill Power, professor of Old Testament at Perkins School of Theology, gave his students four questions for studying any passage of scripture.[20] It is his first question that I want to address in today's sermon. The question? "What does this passage of scripture tell us about God?"

It is my conviction that the way God related to Moses in this account is very much the way he chooses to relate to each of us in this place and this time. Watch with your mind's eye the picture of God's character come into focus. See if this is the same God you have come to know and love.

How many of you have ever seen a burning bush? I'm not talking twigs flaming at a campfire. I'm speaking about a strange phenomenon like the one that captured Moses' curiosity. Curiosity may have killed the cat, but in this story it was the key means for Moses to hear the voice of God. Moses saw the burning bush and noticed that the bush was not being consumed. His curiosity, not his reverence, brought him closer. Verse four gives us the first description of who God is and how he interacts with his people: "When the Lord saw that he turned aside to see, God called to him out of the bush, 'Moses, Moses'! ''

1. What is God like? He is one who speaks to us. God calls us by name; he approaches us. One commentary pointed out that God spoke to Moses from the bush, not once but 13 times.[21] Has God ever spoken to you? Has he spoken as many as 13 times in your life? More times? Less times? At no time?

God has spoken to me. It was never from a burning bush, not even from a flickering flame. But the Spirit of God has called my name on several occasions. One such occasion was my call into ministry. When that word came I knew God wanted me for Christian ministry in his church. I heard his call. But it was not a very loud call. It was a call I could have denied or ignored.

Dr. Fred Craddock, one of my favorite preachers, once remarked, "Why is it that when the Lord calls one into ministry he never speaks loudly enough for anyone to hear?"[22] The validation of God's voice must come from within.

Do you believe that God has spoken to you? Did he answer a prayer? Did he help you with a decision? Did he speak a word of salvation to you that convinced you of its truth? Have you heard the Father say, "You are forgiven!"? Do you recognize the words of God whispered to you from the flaming bush within: "I love you!"?

I am convinced that God speaks to us as surely as he spoke to Moses. I am persuaded that he speaks to us through prayer, through the events of life, even the tragic ones. I believe that God is constantly sharing his truth to us through inner thoughts and insights.

What happened to Moses happens to us. God speaks. We may hear.

2. Our passage reveals a God who knows and cares. Hear again verse seven:

> Then the Lord said, "I have seen the affliction of my people who are in Egypt, and have heard their cry because of their taskmasters; I know their suffering . . . ."

Our God is a God who knows what is happening to his people — the people of Israel, the people of the United States, the people of Iraq, the people of Bangladesh, the people of the Third World. God knows the plight of all his people. And what is implied here is more than mere knowledge. God not only knows of suffering; he also cares about that suffering. Our God is a knowing and caring God.

Paul certainly lived his life with that conviction. In a letter to the church at Corinth he writes:

> Blessed be the God and Father of our Lord Jesus Christ, the Father of all mercies and the God of all comfort, who comforts us in all our affliction, so that we may be able to comfort who are in any affliction, with the comfort with which we ourselves are comforted by God (2 Corinthians 1:3-4).

God knows our problems. He knows our suffering. God empathizes with us. He wants to deliver us from all those things that would defeat us.

How many of you, when a young child (perhaps a son or daughter or grandchild) comes to you with tear-stained cheeks, will keep your distance? How many of you would offer no comfort to a friend who has lost a loved one? How many of you can be unaffected when one you love suffers pain?

Our God, the God of the Hebrews in bondage, knows our pain and he cares about our welfare. He does not keep his distance but comes close enough to wipe away our tears, close enough to embrace us with his loving Spirit.

I ask you plainly, "Have you ever been overwhelmed by suffering or grief or despair only to have a peace come upon you, a peace that passes understanding?'' To what or to whom do you attribute that great gift? Is it inner strength? Is it luck? Is it God?

God speaks. He spoke to Moses from a bush. He speaks to us through people and events, insights and inspiration. God knows and cares. He sees our tears. He remembers our pain. He offers his healing touch.

3. And God also calls. He calls us to special tasks. Remember Moses' call from out of the bush? ''Come, I will send you to Pharaoh that you may bring forth my people, the sons of Israel, out of Egypt.''

Aren't you glad God doesn't call us to tasks like that? Aren't you glad we don't have to face any Pharaohs on behalf of suffering people? Or do we? Maybe that is one of our calls. Or maybe our call is to be a minister, or to change professions, or to be active in a special project, or to teach Sunday school.

God does not call us to one task, but many. Even the man beaten and lying by the side of the road may be our special call at that place, at that time.

I have heard many calls. I remember my call to ministry. I know I heard God's voice. But I'm sure that God has called you as well. How do I know? I overheard God when he gave his call to you. It is the one call he gives loudly enough for everyone to hear. The call is simple but not easy. It is costly, yet rewarding. It is risky, yet with a kind of security. The call is one given to us all: Love God; love neighbor!

Have you heard God give that call? Well, if you haven't, let me speak it clearly so you may hear: ''Love God and love your neighbor as yourself.'' This is our overriding call. This is our first calling. This is the calling before our profession, before our major, before our wants, before our inclinations — love God fully, love neighbor selflessly.

Moses heard God from out of the bush. Where will you hear him? Did you hear him speak today? Do you know he cares? Have you responded to his call?

4. Moses heard another word from the bush. The Spirit of God came ablaze with another great truth: God is with us. For Moses that word of presence came only after his words of excuse and resistance:

> "Who am I that I should go to Pharaoh, and bring the sons of Israel out of Egypt?" [God] said, "But I will be with you . . ."

Long before Moses, God promised to Abraham the gift of his presence. "I will be with you," God assured him. And that promise has never been broken. God has always been present with his people. He was present with them in the promised land and in exile. And he has been with us in the good times and the bad.

Am I wrong? Do you remember feeling God's presence when things were chaotic, when tragedy struck, when failure came your way, when disappointment shook your self-esteem, when the beauty of the natural world caressed you and whispered its lullaby?

Do we have to have a burning bush in the desert to hear from God? Or can we settle instead for the burning bush within, the presence of the living God, the comfort and guidance of his Spirit?

The story of the people of God is the story of God's presence, of God's being with them and God being with us — now and for eternity. Our passage today is far more than a story about a weird happening of Moses at Mount Horeb. It is about everyday occurrences that take place in Dallas, Orlando, Cedar Rapids and San Jose.

It is about God calling us by name, his compassion for our suffering, his daily call to love, his every-moment offer of abiding presence.

Our God, the God of Abraham, Isaac and Jacob, the God of Moses, the God incarnate in Jesus Christ — this same God continues to speak, to know and care, to call us to love and be with us.

But if we are to make full use of God's gracious acts, we, like Moses, must turn aside, draw near; we must listen, we must share our pain, we must respond to God's call and we must decide to abide with the one who offers us his loving presence.

God speaks, cares, calls and abides. So may we, as grateful children, welcome his Spirit as God sets our hearts ablaze!

Endnotes

1. Dimitri of Rostov, quoted in *The United Methodist Hymnal* (Nashville: The United Methodist Publishing House, 1989), p. 466.

2. Bishop Peter Storey, *Address to Academy for Preaching,* January 1991, Nashville, Tennessee.

3. Ibid.

4. Albert C. Outler, *John Wesley* (New York: Oxford University Press, 1964), p. 6.

5. Harold S. Kushner, *When Bad Things Happen to Good People* (New York: Schocken Books, 1981), p. 133.

6. Thomas A. Harris, M.D., *I'm O.K., You're O.K., A Practical Guide to Transactional Analysis* (New York: Harper and Row, Publishers, 1967), pp. 120, 121.

7. Cuthbert A. Simpson, *Genesis,* vol. 1 of *The Interpreter's Bible,* ed. George Arthur Buttrick (New York Abingdon Press: 1952), p. 668.

8. Tim Hansel, *You Gotta Keep Dancin* (Elgin, Illinois: David C. Cook Publishing Co., 1985), p. 35.

9. Gerhard von Rad, *Genesis* (Philadelphia: The Westminster Press, 1961), p. 279.

10. Walter Brueggemann, *Genesis,* in *Bible Commentary for Teaching and Preaching* (Atlanta: John Knox Press, 1962), p. 243.

11. Walter Brueggemann, *Genesis*, in *Interpretation: A Bible Study for Teaching and Preaching,* ed. Patrick D. Miller (Atlanta: John Knox Press, 1982), p. 266.

12. Brueggemann, p. 243.

13. von Rad, p. 319.

14. William Cowper, *The Methodist Hymnal* (Nashville: Parthenon Press, 1964), p. 215.

15. J. Cobert Rylaarsdam, *The Interpreter's Bible,* vol. 1 (New York: Abingdon Press, 1952), p. 864.

16. Ibid., p. 865.

17. Albert Schweitzer, *Out of My Life and Thought* (New York: The New American Library of World Literature, Inc., 1953), p. 138.

18. Ruth Calkin, *Tell Me Again, Lord, I Forget,* as quoted in *Improving Your Serve,* Charles R. Swindoll (Waco: Word Books, 1981), pp. 43, 44.

19. Tom Colvin, as quoted in *The United Methodist Hymnal,* p. 432.

20. William Power, *Lectures on the Old Testament,* Perkins School of Theology, 1968.

21. Terence E. Fretheim, *Exodus,* in *Interpretation: A Bible Commentary for Teaching and Preaching,* ed. Patrick D. Miller (Louisville: John Knox Press, 1991), p. 57.

22. Fred Craddock, *Sermon for North Texas Annual Conference,* Wichita Falls, Texas, May 1983.

A Note Concerning Lectionaries And Calendars

The following index will aid the user of this book in matching the correct Sunday with the appropriate text during Pentecost. All texts in this book are from the series for Lesson One, Common Lectionary. Lutheran and Roman Catholic designations indicate days comparable to Sundays on which Common Lectionary Propers are used.

(Fixed dates do not pertain to Lutheran Lectionary)

Fixed Date Lectionaries *Common and Roman Catholic*	Lutheran Lectionary *Lutheran*
The Day of Pentecost	The Day of Pentecost
The Holy Trinity	The Holy Trinity
May 29-June 4 — Proper 4, Ordinary Time 9	Pentecost 2
June 5-11 — Proper 5, Ordinary Time 10	Pentecost 3
June 12-18 — Proper 6, Ordinary Time 11	Pentecost 4
June 19-25 — Proper 7, Ordinary Time 12	Pentecost 5
June 26-July 2 — Proper 8, Ordinary Time 13	Pentecost 6
July 3-9 — Proper 9, Ordinary Time 14	Pentecost 7
July 10-16 — Proper 10, Ordinary Time 15	Pentecost 8
July 17-23 — Proper 11, Ordinary Time 16	Pentecost 9
July 24-30 — Proper 12, Ordinary Time 17	Pentecost 10
July 31-Aug. 6 — Proper 13, Ordinary Time 18	Pentecost 11
Aug. 7-13 — Proper 14, Ordinary Time 19	Pentecost 12
Aug. 14-20 — Proper 15, Ordinary Time 20	Pentecost 13
Aug. 21-27 — Proper 16, Ordinary Time 21	Pentecost 14
Aug. 28-Sept. 3 — Proper 17, Ordinary Time 22	Pentecost 15
Sept. 4-10 — Proper 18, Ordinary Time 23	Pentecost 16
Sept. 11-17 — Proper 19, Ordinary Time 24	Pentecost 17

Sept. 18-24 — Proper 20, Ordinary Time 25	Pentecost 18
Sept. 25-Oct. 1 — Proper 21, Ordinary Time 26	Pentecost 19
Oct. 2-8 — Proper 22, Ordinary Time 27	Pentecost 20
Oct. 9-15 — Proper 23, Ordinary Time 28	Pentecost 21
Oct. 16-22 — Proper 24, Ordinary Time 29	Pentecost 22
Oct. 23-29 — Proper 25, Ordinary Time 30	Pentecost 23
Oct. 30-Nov. 5 — Proper 26, Ordinary Time 31	Pentecost 24
Nov. 6-12 — Proper 27, Ordinary Time 32	Pentecost 25
Nov. 13-19 — Proper 28, Ordinary Time 33	Pentecost 26 Pentecost 27
Nov. 20-26 — Christ the King	Christ the King

Reformation Day (or last Sunday in October) is October 31 (Common, Lutheran)

All Saints' Day (or first Sunday in November) is November 1 (Common, Lutheran, Roman Catholic)

9 781556 734304